Amistad

Adapted from the junior novelization
by JOYCE ANNETTE BARNES
based on the screenplay by
DAVID FRANZONI and
STEVEN ZAILLIAN

Level 3

Retold by D'Arcy and Evadne Adrian-Vallance
Series Editors: Andy Hopkins and Jocelyn Potter

Pearson Education Limited
Edinburgh Gate, Harlow,
Essex CM20 2JE, England
and Associated Companies throughout the world.

ISBN 0 582 40165 8

First published in the USA by Puffin Books, a member of Penguin Putnam Inc. 1997
Published in Puffin Books 1998
This edition first published 1999
Third impression 1999

TM & © Dreamworks 1997, 1999
Photographs by Andrew Cooper
All rights reserved

Typeset by Digital Type, London
Set in 11/14pt Bembo
Printed in Spain by Mateu Cromo, S.A. Pinto (Madrid)

Published by Pearson Education Limited in association with
Penguin Books Ltd, both companies being subsidiaries of Pearson Plc

For a complete list of the titles available in the Penguin Readers series please write to your local
Pearson Education office or to: Marketing Department, Penguin Longman Publishing,
Penguin Books Ltd, 27 Wrights Lane, London W8 5TZ.

Contents

Introduction

Cinque understood well that he was not a free man now – he and the forty-nine other young Africans, kidnapped from their homes in Sierra Leone.

The *Amistad* was a real Spanish slave ship. It sailed from Havana, the capital of Cuba on 28 June 1839. It was taking some young Africans to work as slaves, but they fought and killed the sailors on the ship. The Africans tried to sail the ship home to Africa but a US ship found them and took them to New Haven in Connecticut on the north-east coast of America. There they faced prison and the courts.

Amistad is now a film, directed by Steven Spielberg. The film is based on the true story of the Africans. Among the famous actors in the film are Anthony Hopkins as the ex-president, John Quincy Adams, and Nigel Hawthorne as the American president of the day. Spielberg filmed *Amistad* in Los Angeles, the Caribbean and at Mystic Seaport in Connecticut. Spielberg also directed the films *Jaws*, *Jurassic Park*, *The Lost World* and *Schindler's List*. The books of *Jaws* and *The Lost World* are also Penguin Readers.

This book is based on the film *Amistad*. It is an exciting story about slavery, the US law and right and wrong. It begins with the bloody fight on the ship and then moves quickly to the US courts of law. The courts must decide: Are the Africans murderers or are they honest men, fighting to be free?

Chapter 1   Escape

The young man lay in darkness in the bottom of the *Amistad*. The ship was moving up and down in the stormy winds. Above him he could hear running feet and loud voices – the men who were trying to sail the ship through the seas.

Cinque couldn't understand the men's language. But he understood well that he was not a free man now – he and the forty-nine other young Africans, kidnapped from their homes in Sierra Leone.*

Heavy chains held them down. The ceiling was so low that they were unable to stand up, almost unable to move. The smell of many bodies so close together was terrible. After months at sea like this, they were weak. But they were also very angry.

Cinque remembered the long sea journey from Sierra Leone to Cuba. In Havana, the capital of Cuba, the kidnappers sold the Africans as slaves. Now the Africans were on a second journey. Spanish sailors were taking them to work in sugar fields for the men who bought them.

But at last, in the middle of this storm, Cinque thought there was a hope of escape. There was a metal spike in a bit of old wood near him. He pulled and pulled at the spike. It was hard work, and it was terribly hot in the ship. The water from his black skin ran down into the wood round the spike. Very slowly, the spike began to move. Just a few more minutes and . . . suddenly, it was out! He pushed the metal into the lock on the chain round his neck and turned it. Left and right, left and right . . . at last, it opened. He was free.

---

* Sierra Leone: A small country on the west coast of Africa.

Cinque unlocked the chains that held the other Africans. And he unlocked all their angry feelings too. Like lions, brave and proud, they followed him up to the top of the ship, into the storm.

They met a Spanish sailor standing at the top of some stairs. He had no time to shout to the others. Cinque took the man's knife and killed him. Next, they broke open a door. Inside the room, they found a large number of long, heavy knives. With angry shouts, they went to find the rest of the men.

The fight was hard and bloody, and the men's screams were terrible. But the Africans could show them no pity: they had to win. Some of the sailors and the ship's captain were trying to escape in a boat. In a minute, Cinque was in front of the captain. Their knives crashed together. The captain was strong but Cinque was younger and stronger. The captain fell to his knees, asking Cinque not to kill him. But Cinque thought, This man has helped to take me away from my home, and he drove his knife through the captain's heart. The Africans had won their freedom.

Cinque now wanted to find two men called Ruiz and Montes. They were the men who bought the Africans as slaves in Havana. During the fight on the *Amistad*, Ruiz and Montes hid in the bottom of the ship. Cinque turned to the others. 'The two men who think that we belong to them,' he said. 'Find them.'

Chapter 2   Towards the East

'I say we kill them both,' Cinque told Yamba, a big strong fighter. He pointed at Ruiz and Montes, who were now standing, chained to posts, at the back of the ship. 'We can sail this ship home without their help.'

Yamba shook his large head. 'We know nothing about sailing. Only those two men can sail the ship.'

The Africans had won their freedom.

Cinque thought about it and finally agreed. Perhaps Yamba was right. The Africans had no idea where they were. But Cinque knew that the sun came up in the east. And he knew, after months at sea, that they were sailing away from the morning sun and from home.

So he went up to Ruiz and Montes. He pointed his knife towards the morning sun and spoke to them in his language. He tried to show them that they must turn the boat round. Ruiz seemed to understand. He took the ship's wheel and the ship began to turn towards the east.

◆

A few days later Cinque was worried. He was the captain of this ship. But really he was the son of a rice farmer in his African village. The richest farmer, yes, but he knew nothing about ships.

Cinque knew that the *Amistad* sailed east towards Africa during the day. But last night, while he was sleeping, a strange

Yamba shook his large head. 'Only those two men can sail the ship.'

noise woke him up. The sails seemed to be moving in an unusual way, and the stars seemed to be turning round in the sky. What did this mean?

Cinque went to Ruiz, pointed at the stars and spoke in his language. Ruiz didn't seem to understand. Cinque lifted his knife to Ruiz's neck. Ruiz angrily took his hands off the wheel and offered it to Cinque. Since Cinque knew that he couldn't sail the ship, he gave the wheel back to Ruiz. But he guessed that at night the ship was not sailing towards Africa. He guessed, but he couldn't be sure.

The next night, Cinque said to Yamba, 'Something is wrong. Look at the stars turning in the sky above us.'

'You worry too much,' Yamba said and he walked away.

Long hot days and weeks passed on the open sea. The other Africans thought that they were sailing back to their families, their farms, their lives. Only Cinque noticed as the moon moved and the ship turned, again.

There was not a lot of food now and very little water. The other Africans began to feel worried and angry. 'When will we get home?' they asked Cinque.

At last, Fala, a small man with very pointed teeth, saw land in front of them. '*Ndogboe!*' he shouted. 'Home!' The others began to shout with happiness. Only Cinque, looking towards the land, knew that they were not home. He told Yamba, Fala, Buakei and a few others to come with him in a small boat.

They soon found water and carried as much as possible towards the beach. Then, as they came out of some trees, they stopped: a large ship was sailing straight towards the *Amistad*. The Africans ran to their boats and started back to their ship, ready to fight again.

Now, men in long boats from the larger ship were coming towards them. Other boats were going towards the *Amistad*. The *Amistad* was getting ready to sail, and then it began to move.

'Hurry,' Cinque ordered the others. 'If we can get to the *Amistad* first, perhaps we can still escape.' Then they heard the sound of guns. The men were shooting at them. Buakei, Fala, Yamba and the others jumped into the water, hoping to swim back to the beach. Cinque jumped in too but he swam towards the open sea. He wanted either to swim back to Africa or to die. Dying was better than becoming a slave.

His strong arms carried him through the water. Still the men followed him. Was there no escape? They were almost on top of him now. He swam down and disappeared.

Down and down . . . Cinque was ready to die. Then, suddenly, he thought he heard a voice, calling him: a woman's voice, his wife's. She was calling him home. Just in time, Cinque turned in the water. When he finally came up, the sun was shining straight into his eyes. A second later, he saw the guns that were pointing at his head.

Chapter 3   In Chains Again

Back on the *Amistad*, Gedney and Meade from the US ship, *Washington*, were asking some questions. 'Where's your captain?' The Africans did not seem to understand. It was even stranger when Gedney and Meade found Ruiz and Montes, wearing chains. They fell to their knees at Gedney's feet, speaking in Spanish. Gedney couldn't speak Spanish. But when he saw the chains in the bottom of the ship, he understood everything and he was very pleased. This was a slave ship, carrying these Africans as slaves. 'If the slaves are mine now,' he thought, 'I can sell them in America and get a lot of money.'

'Sail to Connecticut,' Gedney ordered. 'An American court can decide what happens next.'

◆

Chained together, the Africans left the ship and walked into the town. The people in the town looked at them in surprise. They clearly thought that the Africans were from another world. There was Fala, with his strange, pointed teeth and Yamba, so much taller than them. They think we're murderers or animals, thought Cinque, but he tried to hold his head high and to look straight back at them.

The guards threw the thirty-nine men into one prison and took the young girls to another. In prison, Cinque began to think about the ten Africans who were already dead, either in the

The guards threw the thirty-nine men into one prison and took the young girls to another.

In prison, Cinque began to think about the ten Africans who were already dead, either in the fighting or from illness. What was it all for?

fighting or from illness. What was it all for? And in the darkness, where no one could see him, Cinque dropped his head and hid his face in his hands.

Chapter 4   A Friendly Face

The president of the United States, Martin Van Buren, smiled and waved to the crowd in the small town that he was passing through. The crowd were shouting, 'Van Buren for president! Van Buren for president!' Van Buren wanted very much to become president again. He was enjoying this welcome. So when his secretary, Leder Hammond, shouted the news about the *Amistad* in his ear, he really wasn't interested.

Señor Calderon, an important man from Spain, sat next to the president on the train back to Washington. Calderon was trying to explain the problem of the *Amistad* to the president. 'The *Amistad* is a Cuban ship. It was carrying the slaves from the capital, Havana, to another town.'

'Oh, yes,' said the president.

'The slaves killed almost everyone,' Calderon said. 'Only two Cubans, called Ruiz and Montes, are still alive.'

'Really?' the president replied.

'These two men bought the slaves in Havana,' Calderon explained. 'So the slaves are their property and, since Cuba belongs to Spain, they are Spain's property. The queen of Spain wants you to return the slaves at once.'

When Señor Calderon left, the president said to his secretary, 'Hammond, I'm trying to have a drink after a very long day. There are perhaps three million black people in this country. Why do I have to think about these thirty-nine? If there is a problem, *you* find the answer to it.'

Everyone soon knew the news about the *Amistad* and the slaves, now in an American prison. It was on the front page of some of the newspapers: MURDER AT SEA!

One of the people reading the newspaper story was Theodore Joadson. He remembered the time in the past when he was a slave. Joadson was a free man now, with a good job at the university, but he was one of the lucky ones. Most black people in America were still slaves. When Joadson read the news, he knew that the newspaper was telling only one side of the story. He knew that the 'slaves' from the *Amistad* needed help.

He hurried to see his friend, Lewis Tappan. Tappan was a rich white man but, like Joadson, he wanted slavery to end. He could help because he had a newspaper business.

'These men are probably slaves from the West Indies, don't you think?' asked Tappan.

'No, I don't,' replied Joadson, 'I've seen some of them. They look African; they don't look like slaves. I think they were free men until a short time ago. But the courts will say that they're murderers.'

'Then we must try to tell *their* side of the story,' replied Tappan.

When Joadson next saw one of Tappan's newspapers, the front page told a very different story: THE FIGHT TO BE FREE AT SEA!

Chapter 5   In the Courtroom

The Africans walked to the courtroom in chains. In the courtroom, the Africans, still in chains, felt strange and uncomfortable. The

Joadson was a free man, but he was one of the lucky ones. He knew that the 'slaves' from the Amistad needed help.

The Africans walked to the courtroom in chains.

court was full. People wanted to see the 'murderers'. Most of the crowd were white but there were one or two black faces.

Judge Judson came into the room and sat down. Immediately the US lawyer, William Holabird, began to speak against the Africans. But as soon as he began, Lewis Tappan stood up among the crowd, waving some papers before the judge. 'Sir, I and many others would like to speak *for* these men. At the moment, they have no one to speak for them and they cannot speak for themselves.'

'Mr Tappan, try to remember that you are not a lawyer,' began Holabird with an unpleasant smile, but again he did not finish his sentence. A policeman with two important-looking men pushed through the crowd. The first man was Señor Calderon, from Spain. The second was John Forsyth, a US government secretary.

Now, nobody knew what was happening.

'The slaves,' said Secretary Forsyth, 'belong to Spain, and we must return them to Spain immediately ...'

'Those slaves belong to me and my friend here,' said another voice. Everyone looked round to see who was speaking.

'We, Thomas Gedney and Richard Meade, saved the Spanish ship, *Amistad*, and everything she was carrying. That means the slaves too!'

Secretary Forsyth laughed loudly.

'Do you think you are more important than the queen of Spain?' Judge Judson asked.

There were a few laughs from the crowd. The judge told them to be silent. 'Are there any other people that I need to hear from?' he continued.

Another voice answered, 'The slaves really belong to these two men here.' It was another lawyer, speaking for Ruiz and Montes. Judge Judson looked down into the room full of people. How, he thought, has this case become so difficult? It was almost funny.

A young man standing at the back of the court thought it was very funny. He was a lawyer, too – Roger Baldwin – and he thought he knew the answer to the problem.

♦

Outside the court, Baldwin went up to Lewis Tappan and told him his name and job.

'You're a property lawyer?' asked Tappan, looking at the young man's cheap clothes and untidy hair.

'Yes, if people cannot agree about property, and who it belongs to, they need me. I'd like to help you.'

Tappan and Joadson didn't seem to understand.

'Clearly,' explained Baldwin, 'the problem of the slaves is a problem of who they belong to. Everyone thinks, rightly or wrongly, that the slaves belong to them . . .'

Tappan stopped Baldwin with a wave of his hand.

'I'm sorry, but what we need is a criminal lawyer for these *men*, not a property lawyer for *slaves*,' Tappan said.

Baldwin shook his head. 'You're wrong,' he replied, 'you'll see.' He turned round and walked away.

Chapter 6   People Are Not Property

John Quincy Adams was once the sixth president of the United States. Now he was seventy-two years old. But he was still an important man in the government. He was also a lawyer and a very good speaker. Most days, he just felt old: his hands shook and often he didn't remember things.

Tappan and Joadson went to meet Adams in Washington. Adams shook Tappan's hand but he couldn't remember why they wanted to see him. Something about slaves on a ship. Some trouble. The courts.

'Sir, this is a very important case,' the man called Tappan was saying. 'The queen of Spain says that the Africans belong to her. The president agrees with her. And there are others ...'

Adams suddenly said, 'Do you really think that the president is interested in the queen of Spain or what she wants? I have been president and I know. He is only thinking about one thing at this time of year: how he can become president again.' Adams turned away, 'And I'm sorry but I'm neither a friend nor an enemy of slavery. I won't help you.'

Joadson now decided to speak.

'Sir, I know a bit about you,' he said. 'I have studied what you did as president. And your father, too.'

Adams looked round in surprise.

'But there's still one job for you to do,' Joadson continued. 'There must be an end to slavery. And the fact is that you *are* against slavery. You belong with us.'

Adams didn't get angry.

'You're very clever, aren't you, Mr Joadson?' Adams said quietly. 'But I'll tell you something now. Being clever is useless if you're not polite. Get another man to help you.'

♦

Joadson and Tappan needed a lawyer with a name that was famous in America. Adams was the perfect man, but he was only the first who said, 'No'. They asked other important lawyers to take the case. None of them wanted to do it. Baldwin was their only hope.

While they were having dinner with Baldwin, Joadson spoke about the problem.

'If the courts give the men back to Spain, they'll return as slaves to Cuba. The Cubans will say that the men are murderers and must die. If the courts give the men to the Americans, Gedney and Meade, those two will probably sell them back to Spain. And the men will die.'

'Mr Joadson,' said Baldwin, 'it's much easier than you think. It's the same as land, houses, animals. If you know who they belong to, you have almost won.'

'Animals?' Tappan said. He didn't look pleased.

'Now, in the US,' Baldwin continued, 'the law says that you can only buy or sell slaves if they are born slaves. Is that true?'

Joadson agreed.

'So were they born slaves?' Baldwin asked.

'We don't think so,' Joadson replied. 'We think they were free men in Africa until a few weeks ago.'

'If these men are not Cuban slaves, or anybody's slaves,' said Baldwin, 'if kidnappers took them straight from Africa, then the kidnappers are the criminals. And the people who bought them are also criminals. We can forget murder and all the rest. And we've won.'

15

When Baldwin left, Joadson looked across at Tappan. 'You know, it's possible that he's right,' Joadson said. But he didn't feel very sure. In a US court, nothing could be as easy as that.

Chapter 7 Africans or Cubans?

The Africans were back in court again. This time Baldwin's eyes rested mostly on Cinque. He was the one who killed the *Amistad*'s captain. But his face was brave and his eyes were intelligent. 'Perhaps he's a killer,' Baldwin thought, 'but he looks like a prince.'

Holabird, the US lawyer, stood in front of the jury. He waved the knives that the Africans used on the *Amistad*.

'I cannot begin to describe what these slaves did,' he was saying, 'how bloody . . .'

Holabird's words were strong. But Baldwin knew that this was only half the story. It was his job to tell the Africans' story and it was a very difficult job because the Africans spoke no English, and he, Baldwin, understood not one word of their language.

When Holabird finished, Baldwin stood up.

Untidy as always, looking at the judge and jury over his gold glasses, Baldwin began. 'This case isn't about murder. It's about knowing the difference between one country and another.' Baldwin crossed to stand in front of Fala. 'Open your mouth,' he ordered. Fala looked back at the lawyer, not understanding. Baldwin repeated the order in Spanish. Again, Fala did nothing.

'You see, he doesn't understand,' said Baldwin. 'Stand up,' he said to another African, again in English and Spanish. None of the Africans moved. 'What is your name?' Baldwin asked another. No answer. 'Sir,' Baldwin said to the judge, 'these men understand neither English nor Spanish. That is because they are Africans. They do not belong to the queen of Spain.'

'You have no proof!' Holabird said loudly.

'And I have a bill here,' said Ruiz's lawyer. 'It shows that Mr Ruiz bought these slaves in Havana. It lists their Cuban names. They are black Cubans, born as slaves.'

'Show me a Cuban with teeth like this.' Baldwin put his hand on Fala's mouth and pulled it open. Every eye in the room was on Fala's pointed teeth.

'Yes, Mr Baldwin,' said Judge Judson, 'but do you have any papers – any proof?'

Baldwin stood before the court. 'Sir, I have *them*. These men are my proof.'

Judge Judson looked at the Africans with dislike.

◆

'I thought you spoke quite well,' Joadson told Baldwin outside the court.

'Thank you,' Baldwin replied, but he wasn't sure. He needed proof. Without proof, how could he win the case?

He heard the sound of chains and turned round. The prisoners were coming out of the court. Baldwin watched them as they came closer. As they passed, Cinque gave him a long, hard look and said, '*Ngi kɔlɔ gbɔɔ hi longɔ binde.*'

Baldwin couldn't understand the words, but it was clear that Cinque wanted to say something to him.

The African prisoners moved on. Baldwin watched them as they disappeared down the street towards the prison.

◆

Later that evening Baldwin went to see Cinque. The guards brought Cinque to him in chains. Baldwin held out his hand.

Cinque took Baldwin's hand and pulled it towards his heart. He felt sure that Baldwin was trying to help him.

Cinque took Baldwin's hand and pulled it towards his heart. He felt sure that Baldwin was trying to help him.

'I need to have proof that you're from Africa,' Baldwin said in English.

'You want to show them that we're from Africa,' Cinque said in his language.

'How can you tell me?' Baldwin said. Then he sat down and made a shape with his finger in the dirt on the ground. 'This is my home, here,' he said.

Cinque looked. He understood.

'This is Cuba,' Baldwin continued. He made another smaller shape, a boat and water.

Then Baldwin made the shape of Africa, about half a metre away from the small shape. 'Is this your home? It is, isn't it? Isn't it!'

Cinque looked at this new shape. What did that mean? He stood up and walked away. Then he stopped. He stood in the light of the moon a long way from Baldwin and his shapes.

'Here!' he called out in his language. 'Far, far away. This is my home!'

Baldwin smiled happily. Cinque smiled back.

At last, someone understood.

Chapter 8   Proof

Joadson could not stand up straight. The ceiling was very low. The only light came from his lamp, but he could see the hand and neck chains lying on the floor of the *Amistad*.

Joadson and Baldwin were looking for something. Anything, in fact, that was proof of where the Africans came from. And there was something dark there – he touched it. It was dry blood.

They were all back in court. Baldwin was speaking proudly and holding some old papers in front of the jury.

Joadson closed his eyes. He thought about his mother and father and their journey long ago on a ship like this one.

Suddenly there was a loud noise and a shout. Joadson dropped the lamp and the place became black.

'It's only me,' Baldwin's voice came out of the darkness. 'I fell down some stairs. I haven't found anything yet, have you?'

'No. Light the lamp,' Joadson said. He wanted to go.

As Baldwin lit it, he saw something in the corner. It was a leather bag. Inside there were some papers.

◆

They were all back in court. Baldwin was speaking proudly and holding some old papers in front of the jury.

'These papers have a list of Spanish names on them. Mr Ruiz tells us that these are the names of the prisoners here. We found these papers on the *Amistad*. But they do not belong to the *Amistad*. Look at the name of the ship on these papers. They come from a Portuguese ship, the *Tecora*. We have all heard of the *Tecora*. It's a slave ship that sails between Africa and Cuba!'

Montes and Ruiz looked suddenly worried and angry. Judge Judson gave a long, hard look at Holabird.

Baldwin put the papers in front of the judge.

'These men and women are not slaves. They're not anyone's property and they never have been. Who kidnapped them from their homes in Africa? We don't know that yet. But we know that they're brave men and they fought their kidnappers. So why are they sitting before you, still in chains? Surely it is clear that they must go free!'

Chapter 9   A New Judge

In the president's office, John Forsyth was explaining the problem of the Africans to the president.

'There are two ways that this can end,' he said. 'Either the Africans will die as murderers or they'll go free. Neither of these are good for us. If they die, you'll get a lot of trouble from the people who want to end slavery. But if they go free, you'll get even more trouble from the South: the people who want slavery to continue. They'll be very angry if the Africans go free, and you'll never become president again.'

'Because of this?' Van Buren asked in surprise.

'It's even worse than you think,' warned Forsyth. 'If these Africans go free, every black slave in the country will want to be free. Even a war is possible.'

The president didn't like what he was hearing. But it was true. The newspapers were full of the story of the *Amistad*. In small towns and big cities, in the South and the North, people felt very strongly about it. The problem of slavery was more important now than ever before.

'But there's one hope,' Forsyth continued. 'It seems that Judge Judson wants the slaves to go free. But . . .'

Van Buren looked up hopefully.

'We can get another judge.'

◆

Baldwin was in his office when he got the news. He was so angry that he threw his lamp against a wall.

'The president and his men have got what they want,' he told Joadson. 'Judge Judson will not decide the Africans' case now. It will be Judge Coglin, chosen by Secretary Forsyth. Of course, Coglin will say what the president wants him to say.'

◆

They needed Adams's help. Joadson travelled through the night to see him again. He asked Adams, as politely as possible this time, to tell them what to do.

Again, Adams didn't seem to be interested. But finally he said, 'When I was a young lawyer, I realized that in a court you have to tell a good story. If you tell the best story, you win.'

Joadson was not sure what the old man meant.

Adams continued. 'What is the Africans' story? You and Baldwin have shown *what* they are; they're Africans. But you don't know *who* they are. If you can find out something about them, their story will become more interesting.'

Adams turned away. One thing was clear. Those were the last words that he wanted to say about the *Amistad*.

Chapter 10   James Covey

Baldwin and Joadson now realized that they had to talk to Cinque. Together they thought of a plan.

They had to find someone who knew Cinque's language. So they learned the numbers from one to ten from Cinque. Then, they went down to where the ships came in. There were usually plenty of Africans there. They spent the night moving from table to table in the smoky cafés there. They repeated the numbers in Cinque's language. Finally, they had a piece of luck. A young black sailor, James Covey, heard them and looked up, interested. He had a story to tell, too. When he was a boy, some Spanish men kidnapped him from Africa. But a British ship saved him and the others on the journey. He never went back to Africa. Now, as a man of nineteen, he spoke both English and Cinque's African language perfectly.

Baldwin and Joadson explained what was happening to the Africans. Covey agreed to help them at once.

♦

The next night Cinque sat in prison, listening to Covey. First Covey told his story to Cinque. Then, as Baldwin explained the new problem, Covey repeated his words in Cinque's language. 'Judge Judson wanted you all to go free. But now there is a different judge instead of him.'

'How is that possible?' Cinque wanted to know. In his village, when a man had an important job like that, the job was his for the rest of his life.

'We can't understand it either. But it has happened.' Baldwin stopped to think for a minute. Then he continued. 'I need you to help me. When we return to court, I need you to speak.'

Cinque shook his head. 'I'm not the right person. I can't speak for the others.'

'They say that you can. They say that you're the "big man" here – the most important man. They told me that you – *alone* – once killed a lion. Isn't it true?'

Cinque saw that he had to explain about the lion. 'A lion was killing people in our village,' he began slowly. 'Everyone was afraid.' He closed his eyes, remembering. 'One night it came again, hungry, ready to kill. I had no knife, only a heavy stone. The lion followed me away from my sleeping wife and children. Then I threw the stone as hard as I could. The stone hit the lion and killed it. Everyone was so happy. They gave me a lot of land. But really it was an accident. I was just lucky.'

Cinque looked at Baldwin. He wanted him to understand. 'I'm not a "big man". I was only looking after my family, like any other man.'

Baldwin thought for a moment. 'But what about the other lion, the *Amistad*? Was that an accident too?'

'That wasn't brave,' said Cinque. 'I just wanted to get back to my family.'

'I can help you,' Baldwin said quietly, 'if you will help me. You must tell me how you came here from so far away. Tell us your story.'

Chapter 11   Cinque's Story

Cinque sat in his small prison room with Baldwin and Joadson but he was thinking now of his village in Sierra Leone. He could almost see his big fields, good for growing rice. He could look up at the blue sky and past the fields into the green forest. He could smell rain in the air.

'Early one morning I was in the fields with my brother, Bato. We were planting rice. I left Bato for a short time to go back to the village. My wife and three children will be awake now, I thought. I wanted to have a meal with them before I returned to work.

'I loved to walk along that path, with trees on both sides. I could see the village a long way in front of me. My father's home was in the centre. He was the big man in Mani. He was old but very clever.

'Now I could see my wife, coming out of our house. My young son was following her, playing. Suddenly, someone jumped on me from behind and pulled me down to the ground. They threw a net over me.

'"Bato!" I shouted, but my brother was too far away. He didn't hear me. They pointed a gun at my head and pushed me into the forest.

'We walked for days and nights. We met other kidnappers and their prisoners on the way. One of them was Buakei.

On the ship, every day and night, people became sick and died.

'Finally we came to the high doors of Lomboko, the slave factory. We knew about it already. It was not unusual for people to disappear in our villages. Stories got back to us about what happened.

'They locked hundreds of men, women and children together, like animals waiting to die. Some were sick. Many died. But hundreds were still there. They waited for white men in their white clothes and white hats to sell them. For gold.

'Then they took us on to a great ship. More and more of us. They pushed us, men, women and children, towards a small dark hole. There was a terrible smell of too many people, coming from that hole. I fought against my kidnappers. I didn't want to go into that slave hole. And as they threw me in, I turned and had one last look at Africa, green and beautiful, with the sun coming up in the morning.

'Every day and night, people became sick and died. We had to throw the dead into the sea, where hungry fish swam, waiting. I myself had to do that terrible job.

'There was never enough food or water. We all became weak, specially the very young and the very old. One day, while I was working, I suddenly saw a young mother with her child in her thin arms. She was standing at the side of the ship. For a second she looked at me, her eyes wild. Then, before I could stop her, she jumped into the sea, into the mouths of the great fish.

'Another time, while the "healthy" ones were working, the Spanish sailors pulled some old fishing nets across the floor. They were full of heavy metal balls. They tied fifty or more sick Africans to the nets. I realized what they were doing – *everyone* realized what they were doing. I fought and tried to stop them but it was not possible. I had heavy chains on me. I stood there unable to do anything. The Spanish sailors kicked the nets and all fifty people into the sea.'

Baldwin, Joadson and Covey listened silently. Cinque told the rest of his story about the journey from Africa across the Atlantic to Cuba.

The next day in court Cinque told it again. The room was full of people. But there was no sound and no one moved as he spoke.

Baldwin stood before him in the court and Covey sat next to him, repeating his words in English.

'Finally, after months on water, we came to land. There were so many white people there, all so busy. They took us to another slave prison. It was even bigger than the one at Lomboko. They gave us rice and bananas to eat – as much as we wanted. They wanted to make us fat. We were afraid that they wanted to eat us.

'Then we had to dance for them. They put oil on our bodies until our black skins shone. I soon realized that they didn't want to eat us. They wanted to sell us.'

Here Cinque stopped. His head dropped in front of this room full of people.

'They showed us to people. We felt like animals. We had no clothes on us – only chains. They sold us,' Cinque said, 'to Ruiz and Montes, who put us on a smaller, faster ship – the *Amistad*. They were taking us to work in the sugar fields.'

Cinque told the court about their fight to be free on the *Amistad*. 'I wanted to kill them, too,' he said, pointing at Ruiz and Montes. 'But then we thought that they were taking us home.'

Baldwin moved away from Cinque and returned to his chair. For a few minutes, no one was able to speak. Then Holabird stood up and looked at Cinque with an unpleasant smile.

'That's a most interesting story,' Holabird said. 'But some of it is difficult to understand. For example, why did the Spanish men kill some of the slaves? Slaves mean money. In fact I don't really think that any of your story is true, is it? But like all untrue stories, it was very amusing.'

Holabird turned round and walked away. As Cinque watched him, he felt that there was no hope.

Chapter 12   Captain Fitzgerald Speaks

Cinque returned to his chair, feeling sick and worried. His story was true, every word. But perhaps the lawyers didn't think that it was.

Baldwin now called a second man to speak to the court. His name was Captain Fitzgerald, a British captain who knew about the slave ship *Tecora*. He knew the sort of things that happened to people on that ship.

'Sometimes we stop slave ships,' said Fitzgerald. 'If the kidnappers think that we're going to catch them, they often throw all their prisoners into the sea. Then there's no proof of what they have done.'

'That's what we need now,' said Baldwin, 'proof of what happened, as Cinque describes it, on the *Tecora*.' He pulled out the papers that they found on the *Amistad*. He knew that there was proof in these papers but he said nothing. Fitzgerald took the papers and looked at them.

'But look,' said Fitzgerald suddenly. 'What's this? They changed the number of slaves on the ship. After this date, there were fifty slaves fewer than when the journey began. My guess is that the sailors on the *Tecora* didn't have enough food and water for the journey. So they threw fifty people into the sea.'

♦

Suddenly, Cinque stood up. He called out loudly in English,
'Give us free!'

Cinque wasn't listening to the people in the court now. He was thinking of his wife. He wanted to be with her. And his children, so young. What must they think of their father? He felt sick and so sad. His head was hurting.

Suddenly, Cinque stood up. He called out loudly in English, 'Give us free!'

Everyone in the courtroom turned to look at him. How did he know these words? Time seemed to stop.

'Sir,' Holabird said to the judge, 'he cannot shout like this while . . .'

'GIVE US FREE!'

Judge Coglin seemed too surprised to speak.

'Give us free,' Cinque said once more, quietly, before he calmly sat down.

♦

The next day everyone stood when the judge came into the court. On this day, Judge Coglin had to give his decision. Baldwin was not hopeful. He knew that a US warship, the *Grampus*, was ready down by the water to take the prisoners back to Cuba. The president wanted them out of the country as soon as possible. He had other things to think about.

'I find that I agree with the government in many ways,' said Coglin.

Secretary Forsyth looked pleased.

Baldwin closed his eyes.

'But,' Coglin said, and Baldwin's eyes opened, 'I'm not sure about the information that Mr Ruiz and Mr Montes gave us. Is it true or not? Were these men born in Africa or not?'

Coglin repeated the question. It was clear that this was the only really important thing.

He looked at the prisoners. Finally he spoke. 'Yes, I think they were.'

People's mouths dropped open. They began to shout.

'And so, these people do not belong to the queen of Spain, or to anyone. The government will take them back to their homes in Africa.'

'Hold Mr Ruiz and Mr Montes,' he said to a policeman.

Baldwin jumped out of his chair and threw his arms round Joadson. He pointed to Cinque and shouted to Covey, 'Tell him!'

But before Covey could begin, Cinque smiled. He understood. They were finally, he thought, free.

◆

But he was wrong. That same night Baldwin and Joadson rode again to the prison. They found Cinque talking to Yamba and Covey. They sat down at a table outside the prison. Slowly, Baldwin began to speak. Covey repeated his words.

'Our president, our "big man" wants your case to go to a higher court.'

'What does that mean?' asked Cinque.

'It means,' said Baldwin, 'that a different judge will have to decide the case again.'

'*No!*' shouted Cinque. 'We had a decision. We're free!'

'That's almost true . . .' began Baldwin.

'Almost?' Cinque asked. 'Almost? What sort of place is this? Where you *almost* mean what you say? Where people are *almost* free?'

Cinque pushed Baldwin away from him. These people's promises didn't mean anything. The sound of African voices singing a song came from inside the prison.

◆

John Quincy Adams was at home, looking after his plants, when he got Baldwin's letter.

'Sir, we need you,' the letter read. 'Your country needs you. This case is more important for America than I can describe. We can only win it with your help.'

Adams read the letter quickly. He thought about it for a minute, then he threw it away.

◆

31

They walked into the garden, Adams once a president, and Cinque once a rice farmer. Adams showed Cinque his flowers.

When Baldwin arrived at the prison, Cinque didn't want to talk to him.

'I'm your only hope,' said Baldwin. 'We have to try again.' Cinque didn't even look at him.

Neither of them spoke again until they heard a sound at the door. Baldwin turned and nearly fell off his chair.

It was Adams.

Chapter 13 Adams Has a Plan

Cinque learned that Adams was once the 'big man' of all America. But even before that, he knew that he was important. There was something special in his old eyes, in his calm voice, and in the way that others listened to him. Could Cinque, perhaps, begin to hope again?

During the next few weeks, Adams and Baldwin studied their law books in Adams's library. They didn't often stop to eat or sleep and they spoke little. They had very little time.

A few days before the High Court met to hear the case, Adams decided to talk to Cinque.

Cinque stood at the door of Adams's house in chains, with guards on each side.

'Take those chains off him,' Adams ordered.

They walked into the garden, Adams once a president, and Cinque once a rice farmer. Adams showed Cinque his flowers. Cinque was more interested than any of Adams's other visitors. They sat down to talk, with Covey there to help.

'I want to be honest with you,' Adams said. 'The job in front of us is very, very difficult.'

Cinque said, 'But there are others who can help us.'

'What do you mean?' Adams asked.

'I mean my fathers and their fathers too,' said Cinque. 'I will call into the past, back to when time began, and they will come and help me.'

He stopped and looked hard at the old man. They were both silent. Adams thought about Cinque's words and suddenly a plan came to him. Because of Cinque's words, he knew what he had to say in court.

A week later, the High Court opened to hear the case of the United States against the *Amistad* Africans for the last time.

Chapter 14   At the High Court

Inside the court building in Washington DC, John Quincy Adams was getting ready for the case.

There were nine judges in the court. The judge in the centre was called Judge Taney. Six of the judges were from the South. Three of them had slaves at home. All of them clearly knew what the president wanted.

Adams felt old. His hands shook. But he knew he had to win this case. It was the right thing to do.

The court was full. As Adams stood up to speak, he felt that the world was looking at America.

'This is the most important case that has ever come to this court,' he said. 'It is about all men everywhere. It is about the right and natural way for men to live together.'

Adams went on to talk about the case: the queen of Spain, the president, the *Amistad*, the *Grampus*. Then he said, 'Some people, for example our president, do not think that slavery is wrong. They think it is natural for some men to be slaves. I must say that I cannot agree: it is, instead, natural for men to be free.'

He looked at Cinque, the only African in the court.

'We know how hard a man tries to be free when he is not. He will break his chains. He will kill his enemies. He will try, and try, and try to get home.'

Adams walked over to Cinque and asked him to stand. He wanted everyone to look at the handsome young man. The room was silent.

'This man is black,' said Adams finally. 'We can all see that. But can we also see that he *alone* is the one *great* man in this room?

'In the past, we Americans were not free. We were almost like

34

slaves to the British. Did we think this was right? No, we did not! We fought for our independence. The greatest men of our past are the men who fought and won independence for us. We teach our children about them. They are the fathers of our country. Their pictures are on the walls of this courtroom.' Adams pointed at pictures of George Washington, Thomas Jefferson and Benjamin Franklin. Then he pointed at Cinque. 'In the same way this man here fought against people who wanted to make him their slave. Why do we think he is wrong?'

Adams held up a piece of paper, and his voice grew louder and stronger. 'These great men, Jefferson and Franklin, wrote this, the Declaration of Independence. If slavery is right, what must we do with this important piece of paper? The Declaration of Independence says that all men must be free ... what shall I do with this paper?'

Adams told the court about his conversation with Cinque; and Cinque's words about his fathers' fathers. Then Adams looked up at the pictures on the wall: the pictures of the men who fought for a free America, and pictures of past presidents. There was a picture of his father, the second president of the United States. Then he spoke to the pictures. 'We need to be as strong and wise as you today, so that we are not afraid. Make us brave enough to do what is right. Even if it means war in our country. And if it means war, we hope it will be the last one in our fight for a new America.'

Adams turned and walked past the nine judges.

'And that's all I have to say,' he finished as he sat down.

Outside a light snow started to fall.

◆

The next morning the courtroom was full. They all wanted to hear the decision about the *Amistad* Africans. The judge began to speak.

35

The ship was carrying the Africans back to their homes. Cinque was standing at the front. He was watching the sun, showing them their way.

'The decision of the court is that these Africans are not slaves. They are nobody's property, but are free people ... and so we must return them to their homes in Africa, if that is what they choose.'

And with these words, the judge closed the case.

♦

The chains fell away from Cinque's hands. 'What did you say? What words did you use?' he asked Adams.

'Yours,' was Adams's reply. The two men shook hands. Then Cinque saw Joadson and Baldwin. He walked over to them and offered his hand. 'Thank you,' Cinque said in English. Baldwin took his hand and pulled it towards his heart. '*Bi sie, Sengbe*,' said Baldwin.

Chapter 15   Africa Calls

It was evening at Lomboko, the slave factory where Cinque's terrible journey began two years earlier. A guard was looking out to sea. He could see a ship but he couldn't see what it was. When it came nearer, he saw it clearly. It was British.

It was too late to warn the other guards. British sailors broke down the doors of the slave factory. They shot and killed the guards and the kidnappers. They broke open the prisons. The prisons were full of Africans like Cinque. They too were free!

When everyone was out, the British ship pointed its great guns at the building. In a very short time, it crashed, burning, to the ground.

♦

The American ship, *The Gentleman*, was crossing the Atlantic, carrying the Africans back to their homes.

Cinque was standing at the front. He was watching the morning sun, low in the sky, showing them their way.

He heard his wife again, calling to him. Her voice seemed to come from the land that lay before him, Africa. It was still too far away to see, but it was there, waiting for him.

ACTIVITIES

Chapters 1–5

Before you read

1 Look at the picture on the front of the book. What do you think the book is about? What do you know about this subject?

2 Find these words in your dictionary. The words are all in the story.

   slave   slavery   chain   captain   president   court   judge   jury   law   lawyer   sir   case   proof   property   independence   spike   lion   net   base   direct

   a What does *law* mean in your language? Which other words are about the law?

   b Finish these sentences with other words.

   • Britain has a queen. The United States has a ......

   • On a ship, the ..... is the boss.

   • A thing that belongs to you is your ......

   • A person who belongs to you and is not free is a ......

   • If we write to a man and we do not know his name, we begin *Dear* ......

   • In the past, prisoners often wore metal ..... on their hands and feet.

After you read

3 Are these sentences true or untrue? Correct the untrue ones.

   a Cinque is from Cuba.

   b Cinque and the other slaves kill everyone on the *Amistad*.

   c Ruiz and Montes change the direction of the boat in the night.

   d Gedney and Meade want to sell the slaves in Britain.

   e Theodore Joadson has always been a free man.

   f Roger Baldwin is a criminal lawyer.

Chapters 6–10

Before you read

4 Do you think that the court will free Cinque and the other slaves? What will their lawyers say to help them?

5 Who says these words? Who to? What is happening?

    a 'Open your mouth.'

    b 'Is this your home? It is, isn't it?'

    c 'They'll be very angry if the Africans go free, and you'll never become president again.'

    d 'If you tell the best story, you win.'

6 Why did so many people think that slavery was not wrong? What do you think?

Chapters 11–15

Before you read

7 What do you think Cinque's story is? What has happened to him since he was with his family in Africa?

8 What is the US Declaration of Independence? Who did Americans win *independence* from?

After you read

9 Finish the sentences about these people.

    a John Quincy Adams ...

    b Judge Taney ...

    c Cinque ...

    d Captain Fitzgerald ...

    e Judge Coglin ...

    f British sailors ...

    ... saw a woman jump into the sea with her baby.

    ... burned the prison at Lomboko.

    ... told a policeman to hold Ruiz and Montes.

    ... agreed to be Cinque's lawyer at the High Court.

    ... decided to free Cinque and the others at the High Court.

    ... told the court about the slave ship *Tecora*.

10 John Quincy Adams thinks that the court case is very important. Why?

Writing

11 How does the president want the High Court case to end? Why does he want this? Explain.

12 Write a newspaper report of the High Court case for a newspaper in the same town.

13 You are Cinque. Describe your feelings when you arrive back in Africa.

14 Which parts of the story are the most exciting or interesting for you? Why?

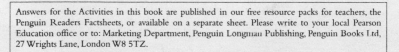